5 SIMPLE STEPS FOR BUILDING A SALES FUNNEL FOR YOUR ONLINE COURSE

WITH FREE AI TOOLS

TABLE OF CONTENTS

BUILDING A SALES FUNNEL FOR YOUR ONLINE COURSE

The online course market is booming, and many coaches, freelancers, and entrepreneurs are taking advantage of this opportunity like never before. If you have some expertise, you can fairly easily create a course, sell it online, and make a solid amount of money.

But many wonder how to go from creating an online course to actually getting customers to purchase it. Building a successful sales funnel for your online course starts with understanding your target market and ends with people enrolling in your course by the dozens.

WHAT COMES FIRST, THE FUNNEL OR THE COURSE?

When you're first considering developing an online course, you may start to wonder how you're going to promote the course, what your offer will be, or how you're going to build your audience. Even before you have a concrete idea of what your course will be, you may start pondering your strategy for getting students.

There are parts of your strategy for launching your online course that may already be in place. For example, maybe you already have a blog already with a burgeoning audience that you can market to. Or, perhaps you're starting from absolute zero and have no idea what to do first.

Don't worry; no matter where you're at in your business journey, you can create a rocking strategy for promoting your new online course.

Let's take a look at how to do that.

STEP 1: UNDERSTAND YOUR TARGET MARKET

Creating an online course is an exhilarating endeavour, but in the midst of this excitement, it's common to focus too heavily on the content and overlook the importance of understanding your audience. The key to a successful course isn't just about what you're offering; it's about ensuring that there's a clear, eager market ready to purchase it. Many course creators make the mistake of diving straight into content creation without first identifying who they are selling to, which can lead to significant challenges down the road.

Understanding your target market is the foundation of your course's success. Before you even start developing your course content, you need to have a clear picture of who your ideal students are. What are their needs, challenges, and goals? What specific problems are they looking to solve? By answering these questions, you can tailor your course to meet their expectations, making it far more appealing and valuable to them.

Knowing your target audience also simplifies the process of reaching them. When you understand who your potential students are, it becomes much easier to find where they spend their time online, what type of content they consume, and how they prefer to engage with it. This knowledge allows you to create more effective marketing strategies, targeting the right people with the right message.

Moreover, a well-defined target market increases the likelihood of conversions. When your course is designed to meet the specific needs of a particular group, they are more likely to see its value and be willing to invest in it. In essence, knowing your audience is not just a step in the process; it's the cornerstone of creating a course that truly resonates and sells.

DEMOGRAPHICS

In order to better understand your target market, you need to find out who they are. The first part of this process is figuring out their demographics.

Get started by answering these questions:

- Where do they live?
- What industry do they work in?
- How much do they earn at their job?
- Where do they spend their time online?
- What are their hobbies?
- What's important to them?
- What scares them?
- What do they want from their life?
- What challenges are they facing?
- What products and services are they interested in?

Really think about the answers to these questions. The more detailed you can be the better chance you'll have of being successful with all aspects of your marketing strategy.

CREATE PERSONAS

A buyer persona is basically a fictional, generalized representation of a customer who is most likely to purchase from you. It's critical to the success of your entire marketing strategy that you understand exactly who your customer avatar is.

When you know who your buyer avatars are you can:

- Determine the social platforms where they are spending their time so you can determine where your business needs to be most active.

- Maximize your exposure and make your marketing dollars more effective by knowing who to target and where to advertise.

- Write copy that better connects with your target customers because you'll have a greater understanding of their pain points, goals, challenges, and successes.

- Develop superior products and services from a place of anticipation of your market's needs.

Creating customer avatars allows you to connect your marketing efforts to your actual customers, and that's a powerful tool.

In order to gather the most accurate and realistic information possible, consider the following techniques:

- Use surveys to gather feedback from your existing customers.
- Reach out to your target market to survey a larger audience base.
- Interview customers as well as leads. Asking why can help you to uncover

the behaviors that drive their purchase decisions.

Having multiple avatars is expected, especially if you're offering more than one product or service. Tackle your avatars one at a time and start with the avatar that will bring the most profit to your business. You can also use this information to really develop your niche and position yourself to be the best option within that niche.

You can also consider creating negative personas, which can be as helpful as customer personas. Knowing who you don't want can make it easier to determine who you do want as a customer. Be sure to focus on reasons they weren't a good fit for your business rather than their personal characteristics.

5 STEPS TO DEVELOPING YOUR CUSTOMER AVATAR

1. **Identify Your Persona's Demographics**: Start by listing the basic demographic details of your target audience. Use relevant questions to determine the key traits of your ideal customer, often referred to as your "avatar." Consider factors like age, gender, occupation, income level, education, and location.

2. **Explore Their Psychographics**: Go beyond demographics by delving into the psychographic traits of your buyer personas. This involves understanding their deeper characteristics, such as their attitudes, interests, values, and lifestyles. These insights will give you a more comprehensive view of what drives their decisions.

3. **Give Your Avatar a Name**: To make your avatar more relatable, assign it a name. This simple step can help humanize your persona, making it easier for you and your team to

reference and connect with the specific characteristics of each avatar.

4. **Create a Detailed Dossier**: Personalize your avatar further by compiling a dossier that includes their name, demographic and psychographic information, and a brief backstory. Include a stock photo that visually represents your avatar, helping to bring them to life.

5. **Craft a Narrative**: Write a narrative that describes your persona's journey to discovering your product or service. Outline what challenges they were facing, what they were searching for, and what they hoped to achieve. This narrative will help you understand their motivations and how your offering fits into their story.

Developing customer avatars helps to hone your messaging and make it more effective. Knowing your target audience is key to an effective marketing strategy.

STEP 2: BUILD AN EMAIL LIST

Building and growing your email list is crucial for two key reasons:

First, selling your course to cold traffic—people who have never heard of your brand, your course, or you—is significantly more challenging than selling to those who are already on your email list. The people on your email list are considered warm leads. They're familiar with you, they trust you, and they've shown interest in what you're offering. This level of familiarity and trust makes it much easier to convert them into paying customers when you launch your course.

Second, your email list is an asset that you own entirely. Unlike social media platforms or other online channels where you can be banned, blocked, or have your reach restricted, your email list is yours to keep. This ownership gives you direct access to your audience without interference, making it an incredibly valuable marketing tool.

In essence, your email list is the lifeblood of your course marketing efforts. As you grow this list and consistently provide value to your subscribers, you're building a relationship based on trust. Over time, you can offer your course to your list, knowing that they are more likely to be receptive and interested. This approach is part of a long-term strategy that has proven to be highly effective.

If the idea of building an email list feels overwhelming, don't worry—you're not alone. It's a process that can be broken down into manageable steps. With a clear plan and consistent effort, you can develop a robust email list filled with warm leads who are eager to buy your course.

CREATE A WORTHWHILE LEAD MAGNET

Building an email list sounds like a pretty simple task but most people tend to be pretty guarded about handing out their email addresses these days. In other words, they aren't just going to give up their email address because you ask really nicely.

The key is to offer them something really valuable in return. That's where your lead magnet comes in.

Let's back up a bit. What is a lead magnet anyway?

A lead magnet is an offer, a gift really, that you are going to give away to your target market just for giving you their contact information. This is why knowing your target market is step one. You have to know what they want.

Remember that the bigger picture in all of this is to build a trusting relationship with your audience so they come to you when they are ready to purchase. That means, your lead magnet needs to be something of great quality in order to keep the relationship thriving.

So, how do you create a lead magnet that is so irresistible to your target market that they're willing to give up their contact information?

First, you should keep in mind that whatever resource you choose should be easy for your audience to consume and easy-ish for you to create. You may spend a couple of hours creating this item for your lead magnet but keep in mind you'll be using it over and over.

Here are some examples of great lead magnets:

- Cheat sheet

- Ebook
- Abbreviated course
- Video series
- Infographic
- Tutorial

The best lead magnet is one that will resonate with your audience. Figure out a topic that is acutely important to your personas and then create a resource to match it.

You can leverage the latest AI technology, like ChatGPT, to generate high-quality ideas for creating an effective lead magnet that truly resonates with your target audience. With its advanced language processing capabilities, ChatGPT can help you brainstorm innovative concepts and pinpoint what will attract and engage potential customers.

By tapping into this AI tool, you can quickly explore a wide range of lead magnet ideas, from e-books and checklists to webinars and mini-courses, all tailored to the interests and pain points of your audience. ChatGPT can also assist you in refining your ideas, ensuring that your lead magnet offers real value and addresses the specific needs of your prospective students or clients.

Route to chat gpt

Additionally, ChatGPT can help you craft compelling copy for your lead magnet and related landing pages, making sure that your messaging is clear, persuasive, and aligned with your brand voice. By using this cutting-edge AI technology, you can streamline the process of creating a lead magnet that not only captures attention but also converts visitors into loyal subscribers and, eventually, paying customers. This approach allows you to focus more on the strategic aspects of your business while letting AI handle the creative brainstorming.

GETTING LEADS TO YOUR MAGNET

Once you've created a lead magnet, you need to get it in front of the right people and get them to convert, or take advantage of your magnet in exchange for their contact information.

So, let's go back to our personas once again and remember where our target market spends its time online. That's where you want to offer your lead magnet.

Try these out to get started:

- Websites and forums they're active in
- Facebook groups they participate in
- Influencers they follow on social media
- Podcasts they enjoy
- Email newsletters they subscribe to
- Blogs they read
- YouTube channels they subscribe to

By targeting the places where you know your target market is spending their time, you'll be able to easily drive them to your magnet.

You can also use SEO on your website and blog to drive organic traffic to your lead magnet or PPC advertising.

The lead magnet itself is simply a landing page connected to CMS (content management system) so you can collect the email addresses and promptly send out the magnet. Don't forget to also send them a nice thank you email for signing up.

STEP 3: START CREATING CONTENT

Now you are collecting email addresses and sending your lead magnet to your new subscribers. Your course probably isn't live yet, so you're going to need to nurture your list for a bit while you're getting it ready.

You can do this with content. Blogs, emails, newsletters - these are all great ways to keep your leads interested, keep building trust, and develop your relationship.

BLOG POSTS

Blog posts are a great way to keep nurturing your list. On one hand, you can link them in emails and provide valuable information to your new subscribers so you stay relevant until you make your offer. On the other hand, you can optimize the articles for SEO, which can bring even more traffic to your blog, where you can also place a landing page for your lead magnet.

Blog posts are a great way to provide your audience with information that will help to solve their problems. If you have already helped them through some of their difficulties, when you make the offer for your course, they will feel much more comfortable signing up.

Blog posts also make great social media content and can open up conversations about your products and common problems among your audience.

EMAILS AND NEWSLETTERS

Emails and newsletters are also a great option. You can keep nurturing and marketing to your email list on a regular basis to keep your audience captivated by what you have to offer them.

SOCIAL MEDIA

Don't try to maintain an account on every social media platform out there. Remember, you know where your customers are spending their time. Choose 1-2 platforms where your target audience is most likely to be and start accounts for your business.

You can post links to your blog articles and share information you find relevant. You can also interact with your audience in forums and in the comments section, and use the information you gain to refine your personas and learn new ways to reach your audience.

STEP 4: BUILD YOUR COURSE

You've probably already been building your course at this point, as you've been working on the first three steps. Building an online course can be challenging and you can't go wrong with lots and lots of planning.

Because this is not a book about building an online course, but rather creating a funnel for your online course, we won't delve into a lot of depth here. Still, let's look at the basics.

CHOOSE YOUR COURSE TOPIC

It goes without saying that your course topic should be something that you're not only knowledgeable about, but also something that you're passionate about. If you have no passion for your topic, it will come through in your teaching and students will find your course less than engaging.

You don't have to have any special knowledge or degree in order to have a winning online course. Pull from the skills, talents, and life experiences that you already possess. As long as there are people who want to learn what you want to teach, you will be able to monetize your topic.

If your course doesn't appeal to your target audience, you'll have a hard time selling it. People are looking for a transformative experience from an online course. They want to go from their current reality to the future they've been dreaming about.

One simple way you can zero in on a course topic is to start a list of your passions/interests, skills, and experience. Try breaking it out into three columns.

Interests Passions	Skills	Experience

Remember, you're looking for a topic that people will be motivated to pay money to learn about.

NARROW DOWN YOUR IDEAS TO THOSE WITH HIGH-MARKET DEMAND

Don't spend a minute creating a course if you're not certain there will be a demand for it in the marketplace.

Once you've settled on a course topic, do some research in the market to see what the demand for your course will be. You might be hesitant about a course topic because you think there's too much competition, only to find out that your particular niche has high demand and little competition, making it well worth investigating further.

There are a few ways to check for the demand for a particular topic:

- Are people searching for it and asking questions that would be answered by the course?
- Are there gaps in what the competition is offering that you could squeeze into?
- Will someone be willing to pay money to solve the problem that your course solves?

If the answer to these questions is yes and you can fill gaps left by the competition, odds are you have a winning idea.

Use tools like Google Trends to see if people are searching for the topic of your online course. You can also enter keywords to get some insight into exactly how many people are searching for the course ideas you've come up with.

This is also a nifty way to find ideas for lead magnets you can use to build your email list.

Here are a few other things you can consider when trying to narrow down your course topic:

- What exactly are people asking about your course topic?
- What's the competition offering?
- Can you offer a fresh take on a popular topic?
- How can you present your topic so it appeals to a different audience?

Engage with your audience to gain more insight about their challenges and if they'd purchase a course that could help overcome them.

CREATE COMPELLING LEARNING OUTCOMES

Learning outcomes are a critical piece in the success of your online course. People want to know exactly what they're going to learn about in your course and how that information will impact the problems they're trying to solve.

Remember, people who purchase online courses are looking for a transformation from their current reality to their awesome future. If your potential students don't know how your course is going to help them, they won't be very likely to enroll.

Learning outcomes clearly define what the student will be able to do, know, and feel by the time they are finished with the course.

- What new knowledge will they obtain from the course?
- What skills will they be able to demonstrate?

- How will they feel about the subject once they've completed the course?

Learning outcomes also help to ensure that the people joining your course are in the right place which contributes to higher satisfaction and completion rates as well as fewer refund requests.

GATHER YOUR CONTENT AND STRUCTURE YOUR COURSE

This is the point where many course creators get stuck. There are so many things you want to cover in your course, and those things lead to other things, and before you know it, you have way more content than you need and it's a jumbled mess.

There is no magic bullet to the length of your course. It doesn't have to be a certain length in order to be successful. It has to be long enough for the student to achieve the learning outcomes that you promised in your marketing.

Those being said, make sure that each of your learning outcomes has content aligned to it.
Then start grouping together content with similar themes into modules and structuring the content within those modules into a logical progression to create a sequence of lessons.

It's helpful to create an instructional design storyboard. This helps to keep your course focused and assures you hit all of the important points in your training.

You'll also want to spend some time structuring your course and your overall academy because you'll likely create more courses related to the same subject. For example, what media do you plan to use? Will there be some written material as well as video material? Planning this out ahead of time will really help you to stay on track.

From here, you'll create a course outline and plan individual lessons. A structured path to delivering content to your students helps them to absorb the material and feel like an expert on the subject by the time they're done.

Consider these points:

- What are the basics that your students already know?
- What do they need to learn?
- What's the best way to teach it to them?

Then you can determine the most engaging and effective way to deliver the information to your students.

BUILD A PRE-LAUNCH AUDIENCE

Building a pre-launch audience is a critical strategy for ensuring a successful online course launch. By engaging with potential students before your course goes live, you create a community of interested individuals who are primed and ready to enroll as soon as your course becomes available. This early engagement can significantly boost your initial enrollment numbers and set the tone for long-term success.

Why a Pre-Launch Audience Matters

A pre-launch audience allows you to generate buzz and anticipation for your course. It's much easier to sell to an audience that already knows, likes, and trusts you than to start from scratch on launch day. By cultivating this audience ahead of time, you not only increase your chances of a strong launch but also gain valuable insights into what your potential students are looking for, which can help you fine-tune your course content and marketing messages.

Steps to Building Your Pre-Launch Audience

Create a Lead Magnet:

The first step in building a pre-launch audience is to offer something of value for free. This could be an e-book, a webinar, a checklist, or a mini-course related to your main course topic. A lead magnet attracts potential students by providing them with useful content in exchange for their email address. This allows you to build a targeted email list of people who are genuinely interested in your course.

Create a Landing Page:

A well-designed landing page is essential for capturing the contact information of your potential students. This page should clearly highlight the benefits of your lead magnet and make it easy for visitors to subscribe. The landing page serves as a focal point for your pre-launch efforts, directing traffic from your content marketing, social media, and other promotional activities to a single place where they can sign up and learn more about your upcoming course.

Leverage Content Marketing:

Use your blog, YouTube channel, podcast, or social media platforms to create content that is aligned with your course topic. Regularly share valuable insights, tips, and resources that demonstrate your expertise. This not only helps to attract your ideal audience but also positions you as a trusted authority in your niche.

Engage with Your Audience:

Interaction is key to building a loyal pre-launch audience. Engage with your followers on social media, respond to comments, and participate in relevant online communities and forums. You can also use surveys or polls to involve your audience in the course creation process, asking for their input on what they'd like to see in your course. This creates a sense of ownership and investment among your audience.

Use Email Marketing:

Once you've built an email list, nurture your subscribers with a series of emails that provide value and build anticipation for your course. Share behind-the-scenes updates, exclusive content, and sneak peeks of what's to come. As your launch date approaches, gradually shift your focus to the benefits of your course and how it can help them achieve their goals.

STEP 5: LAUNCH YOUR OFFER

Once you have an email list and a course in place, you can start launching your offer. Don't get caught up in how many people you have on your email list. You've already built that part of your funnel, so you're going to keep adding addresses all of the time.

You will definitely want to segment your email list according to who you've already sent the offer to and who bought the course and who didn't. You'll learn more about that later.

There are three main stages of an online course launch:

- Pre-Launch
- Launch
- Post Launch

Let's go through each stage, step by step.

PRE-LAUNCHING YOUR ONLINE COURSE

Pre-launching your online course entails a lot of what's already been covered. For example, if you're a coach of some kind and are offering one-on-one coaching but want to make the leap to course creation, this is where you're going to start.

- The first thing you'll decide on is your target audience for your course. You want to make sure you create the content that will compel them to action.

- Find out what your target audience already knows about a particular subject and how you plan for your course to fill in the gaps.

- Research your competition to see what they're offering so you can do it better.

Dig into their problems and pain points.

- Survey your target audience so that you're clear on what specific problems they're trying to solve.

- Create a social media strategy so you know which platforms to focus on.

- Watch for social media mentions regarding your online course topic. Try to join in on the conversation and ask participants detailed questions so you will have a clear idea of the problems they have and the solutions they are seeking.

- Share details about your course in the Facebook groups you're participating in but don't spam the group members. Subtle hints regarding your launch will work best.

Review your course's goals and learning outcomes.

Reviewing your online course as you're getting ready to launch will help you stay on track to not only offer a quality course to your customers, but also market it for maximum results.

- Review the content you already have and determine what should be included with your course and what could be used as marketing materials.

- Plan your course according to step 4 and outline your course and modules.

- Establish a consistent brand voice throughout your course and content to create a seamless, sincere experience for your audience. This will increase trust with your audience for your course.

PRICING YOUR ONLINE COURSE

There is no exact science for pricing your online course. Ultimately, the price you put on your course will come down to the value you place on what you've created. Yet, you have to also consider what else is available that is similar within the market. You definitely don't want to price yourself out of the market.

Here are some tips for pricing your online course so you can deliver the best product while also making a profit.

1. Focus on Value.

The way customers perceive price is just as important as the price itself. Your customer will attach a value to your course and the price you put on it is one way that they will do that. If you price it too cheaply, your customer may form a perception that the information has little value.

By providing quality content and positioning yourself as an expert in your industry you can boost the value of your course. You can also consider these tips for boosting the value of your course:

- Highlight the benefits over the features. Benefits are what your customer is going to get out of your course. Features are what the course has to offer. By focusing on the benefits, you can dial into your customer's pain points and explain how your course can put them on track to the future they want or make their life better.

- Help them see it as an investment. Travel on a journey with your audience from where they are now to where they will be once they have completed your course. Highlight the fact that the price they will pay for your course is an investment in their future by saving them time, helping them lose weight, achieving financial security, etc.

- Give access to an exclusive community. You can also boost the value of your online course by creating a community online for members only for your customers. This is a group of people who are all taking your course or have taken your course, who can then build relationships with one another to ask questions and bounce ideas.

- Provide extra support. By providing specialized coaching, you can offer extra support and reassurance on a one-on-one basis. If the thought of meeting with each student one-on-one is daunting, consider some small group chats for people who are experiencing similar issues.

- Create downloadable resources. By allowing students to download your lessons, you give them the convenience of learning any time and any place. You can also give them downloadable templates, checklists, or e-books to help them reach their goals.

- Provide a certificate of completion. There's just something about having a certificate with your name on it that says you've accomplished something that feels good. Certificates are also highly valued by potential employers.

Pricing your online course to create value for the customer means over-delivering on expectations and ensuring your students succeed.

2. Avoid *Race-to-the Bottom* Pricing.

It can be intimidating to enter the online course market. It may seem like there are a million new courses popping up every day. You will be tempted to offer your course at a rock-bottom price in order to have an advantage over your competition.

Don't fall for it - it's a trap! Here are some of the pitfalls of pricing your course this way.

- It takes the same amount of work to make a value-packed course. You're going to have to put in the same amount of effort no matter what you charge for your course. You'll still have to acquire and nurture leads and do the same amount of marketing. A higher-priced course may require a more detailed funnel but in the end, the extra effort will be worth the extra income you could make.

- A lower price might cause you to lose interest in finishing your course. It's hard to get motivated to get your course finished knowing you're going to make less money. Especially since a lower price doesn't mean people will be lining up for your course.

- You won't have as much to spend on marketing. Selling your course at a

really reduced price means you won't
have as much profit to reinvest into
marketing the course.

More than likely, you have valid reasons for
charging a reduced price for your course.
Try to change your point of view from
reasons you *can't* charge a premium price to
reasons why you *can*.

Sometimes, it takes a real mindset shift to
avoid underpricing your course. Remember,
there's an audience that really wants what
you're teaching and your method is going to
resonate with them. Your course will help
people deliver on the promises they've made
to themselves and they are willing to pay for
the opportunity.

3. Offer Payment Plans.

If you price your course at a premium, it
might be a good idea to offer a payment
plan. Payment plans can increase the sales of

your course because it gives an option for those who really want to take the course but can't quite commit to your price point in one lump sum.

If your price point is $300 or more, consider giving a payment plan option to spread the cost out.

There are great benefits to offering a payment plan:

- You can charge more. Because offering a payment plan makes your course more accessible to those who can't pay in one lump sum, you can actually charge a little more for your course. Especially when you believe in the value of what you're offering.

- Better sign-up rates. If you offer a payment plan, more sign-ups are inevitable as more people can afford your course.

Of course, before you decide to offer a payment plan, you should consider whether your course is long enough to break into at least three monthly installments. You don't want customers to feel like they didn't get enough value in return for what they paid.

Also, you need to make sure your course delivers on the promises you've made. If the customer feels like the course has value, they will continue making the payments and not cancel and quit the course.

PROMOTING YOUR LAUNCH

Even if you've launched your course, no one is going to know to sign up unless you promote and market your launch. But here's the thing. You don't have to finish creating your course before you can successfully launch.

Pre-selling your online course is actually a great way to test the waters to see if your target market is willing to spend their hard-earned dollars on your course and if you're going to get enough recurring revenue from your course.

If the pre-sell is successful, you'll have some extra money to invest in creating and marketing your course.

Consider enrolling beta testers for your course. These are people you trust that need what you're offering. You can pre-sell your course to them for a discounted rate so you can get their feedback about what works and what doesn't. This is a great way to get in-depth feedback with a soft launch to get you ready for the real deal.

Once you've gotten some feedback from the beta testers, you can tweak your course accordingly. As you make the changes, continue to consult with your beta users to make sure you're on the right track.

Start stirring up the excitement for your launch. There are a lot of great ways for you to promote your launch.

Consider implementing some of these great ideas:

- Write about your course in your blog. You can take a small part of your course and go in-depth in a blog article so you show your audience that you're an expert.

- Use SEO to attract new, organic traffic to your site.

- Have some of your beta testers give testimonials about your course. This is a great thing to include on your sales page or course site.

- Consider using a mini-course as a lead magnet for your real course. Then, you can use any comments or questions to fine-tune your course content.

You definitely want to create an email sequence to build excitement for your launch. This is when that email list you've been diligently building is going to shine. An automated email sequence can start out building excitement for your course and gradually make your offer.

If your subscribers have already trusted you enough to sign up for your email, they'll likely be excited to hear about your course.

Consider these types of emails in your launch sequence:

- Your first online course launch email should be aimed at building your subscriber's anticipation, so they're excited to hear about your course.

- Next, you can give the details about exactly what your course covers. Let them know the lessons, modules, and specific learning outcomes they can achieve.

- In the following email, you can address FAQs. For example, payment plans, refund/cancellation policy, as well as information about the course itself.

- An email that provides a sneak peek into the course is a great way to create some buzz. Consider a promotional video or sales letter.

- Offer a bonus in the next email. This could be a free gift, extra module, or discounted price if they use a promo code or sign up by a certain date.

- Send an email with social proof, like the testimonials from your beta group.

- Schedule a live webinar or social media live that you'll host which will include some sort of special gift or bonus for sign-ups.

- Finally, send an email laying out the reasons (benefits) they should purchase the course during the launch. Focus on the transformation.

Don't forget to segment your email list as you go. You don't want to keep sending the same emails to the people who signed up as the people who didn't.

LAUNCHING YOUR COURSE

The big day has finally arrived and it's time to launch your online course. Preparation and planning will go a long way to making this day run smoothly while signing up as many subscribers as possible.

While there are probably as many ways to launch an online course as there are online courses, here's a list of things you can do to have a successful launch:

1. Prepare two emails for your subscribers. Send one the morning of the launch to announce the launch. Send another later in the afternoon or evening to remind them about any special gifts, discounts, or bonuses that they will miss out on if they don't sign up soon.

2. Host a live event on social media or via webinar to demonstrate the value of whatever problem your course is solving. Let them see you're an expert who can be trusted to get them through their current reality to their perfect future.

3. Host a Q&A for anyone who's on the fence about investing in your course.

POST-LAUNCH

After you've launched your course, you'll need to continue to nurture your new students to prevent churn. You want to ensure that they are getting more than they expected in order to reduce drop-outs and refund requests.

Try these tips:

- Develop an onboarding process that welcomes them and clearly explains how to navigate and use the course to its full potential.

- Create a thriving community that prevents customer churn and takes some pressure off of you to be everything for everyone. Encourage students to interact with one another and they will help and encourage each other.

- Continue engaging with your students. Launching a course is the beginning of your relationship with this customer. Check-in to make sure things are going well and offer additional support to prevent abandonment. This is probably a great place for another email sequence.

- Encourage students to share their successes within the community you've provided and how they implemented what they learned in your course. Keep the community motivated by continuing to engage and motivate others in the group.

FINAL THOUGHTS ABOUT BUILDING A SALES FUNNEL FOR YOUR ONLINE COURSE

Building a sales funnel for your online course sounds complicated but it's really not. All that a sales funnel does is direct your target audience to your product so they can buy it.

At the top of the funnel, you're pinpointing your target audience and giving them value-packed content to solve a problem they are experiencing. This starts a relationship and builds trust. Then, you're going to collect email addresses from people who are interested in what you have to offer in your free content. They want more from you. Create a landing page to collect their email address in exchange for some sort of lead magnet.

Finally, launch your course. Then refine it, make it better, and launch it again.

That's it! Now get out there and build a funnel that crushes it.

LIST OF FREE AI TOOLS TO HELP BUILD YOUR FUNNEL

❖ Website:

If you're looking to build high-converting websites, Gamma.app stands out as one of the best tools available today. This platform is designed to help you create visually stunning, user-friendly websites that not only attract visitors but also convert them into customers.

Gamma.app offers an intuitive interface that makes the website-building process seamless, even for those with minimal technical expertise. It provides a wide range of customizable templates and design elements, allowing you to craft a website that perfectly aligns with your brand's identity.

One of the key strengths of **Gamma.app** is its focus on performance and user experience. The platform ensures that your website loads quickly, is mobile-responsive, and offers a smooth browsing experience.

Moreover, **Gamma.app** integrates with various marketing and analytics tools, enabling you to track user behavior, run A/B tests, and fine-tune your website based on real-time data. By using Gamma.app, you can create a website that not only looks great but also drives results, turning casual visitors into loyal customers.

Route to gamma.app

❖ Create Logo

When it comes to creating a professional logo, LogoAI.com is one of the best tools you can use. This AI-powered platform simplifies the logo design process, allowing you to generate high-quality, customized logos in just a few clicks. With LogoAI.com, you can explore a variety of design options tailored to your brand's identity, ensuring your logo is unique and visually appealing. The platform's user-friendly interface and intelligent design algorithms make it easy for anyone, regardless of design experience, to create a logo that stands out and represents your brand effectively.

Link to logoai.com

❖ Content automation:

Scribe is a powerful tool designed to simplify the documentation of processes by automatically capturing and organizing your workflow into visual guides. Whether you're creating training materials, user manuals, or step-by-step instructions, Scribe makes the process effortless. As you work through your tasks, Scribe records each step, generating detailed guides complete with text, links, and screenshots instantly.

This automation saves you time and ensures consistency in your documentation, making it easier to share knowledge across your team or organization. The visual guides created by Scribe are easy to follow, reducing the learning curve for new employees or users. Additionally, Scribe allows for easy editing and customization, so you can refine the guides to meet specific needs or branding requirements.

By using Scribe, you can streamline the process of documenting workflows, ensuring that all important procedures are clearly communicated and accessible, ultimately improving efficiency and productivity within your team.

Route to scribe

Creating Landing pages

Creating eye-catching landing pages is made simple and effective with the powerful features of System.io. This all-in-one marketing platform provides an intuitive drag-and-drop builder that allows you to design visually appealing landing pages without any need for coding skills. Whether you're promoting a product, capturing leads, or driving traffic to a specific offer, System.io equips you with the tools to create high-converting pages that grab attention and engage visitors.

System.io offers a wide range of customizable templates, enabling you to tailor your landing pages to perfectly match your brand's style and message. The platform's design tools let you incorporate stunning visuals, compelling text, and strategic call-to-action buttons, all optimized for mobile devices to ensure a seamless user experience across different screen sizes.

Get Instant Access

CONCLUSION

Regardless of where you are in your journey, crafting a successful online course promotion strategy is entirely achievable. Whether you're starting from scratch or have some elements already in place, the key lies in a strategic approach that addresses your audience's needs and builds excitement around your course.

Begin by deeply understanding your target audience—their pain points, goals, and preferences. This knowledge will guide not only your course content but also your marketing efforts, ensuring that your messaging resonates and attracts the right students. Building anticipation is another crucial element; by engaging potential students early on and nurturing them through consistent communication, you create a buzz that can drive significant interest before your course even launches.

Leveraging content marketing is an essential strategy for establishing authority in your niche and generating organic traffic. By providing valuable insights and resources, you position yourself as a trusted expert, which helps in converting visitors into students. Additionally, social proof, such as testimonials and case studies, plays a powerful role in persuading potential students to enroll, as it builds trust and demonstrates the effectiveness of your course.

With a well-thought-out and executed plan, you can not only launch a successful online course but also create a sustainable educational offering that continues to grow and impact students long after the initial launch.

www.ingramcontent.com/pod-product-compliance
Lightning Source LLC
Chambersburg PA
CBHW082239220526
45479CB00005B/1280